NEW MIND!
NEW YOU!

WAYLYN HOBBS, JR.

NEW MIND! NEW YOU!

Copyright © 2005 by Waylyn Hobbs Jr.

ISBN: 0-9770398-2-X

Published by

LIFEBRIDGE
BOOKS
P.O. BOX 49428
CHARLOTTE, NC 28277

Printed in the United States of America.

DEDICATION

*This book is dedicated to my mother,
Lillian Hobbs-Bigby. Thanks for all the love
and support any son could ask for.*

ACKNOWLEDGMENTS

*To my family—the best family a person
could ask to be a part of. My wife Donna,
thank you for all your love and support. My
wonderful children, daddy loves you guys! The
Coney Island Cathedral Church, thanks for being one
of the worlds greatest churches. In loving memory
of my father, Waylyn Hobbs, Sr., and my
father in the ministry, Dr. J. J. Howell.*

CONTENTS

INTRODUCTION   7

HOW TO MEMORIZE SCRIPTURE   9

CHAPTER 1   IT STARTS IN THE MIND   15

CHAPTER 2   IT'S TIME FOR NEW THINKING   39

CHAPTER 3   THE GREAT TRANSFORMATION   53

CHAPTER 4   THE GUILT TRIP   69

CHAPTER 5   THE ART OF INTIMIDATION   83

CHAPTER 6   IT'S NOT AN ILLUSION   97

CHAPTER 7   THE KEYS TO MIND RENEWAL   113

CHAPTER 8   IT'S ALREADY DONE   129

INTRODUCTION

This is not an ordinary book. Instead it written to become a turning point in your Christian walk and a dynamic life-changing experience.

I say this because you are about to be challenged to memorize select passages of God's Word. These 52 verses have been specifically chosen to give you exactly what you need to live a victorious life.

In each chapter you'll discover biblical principles regarding *why* we must have a transformed mind and *what* God tells us concerning the power of our thoughts.

Most important, the book begins by giving you practical steps to scripture memorization. When the Word becomes buried deep within your heart, you begin to think as God thinks and your actions reflect His will and purpose for *you!*

When faced with difficult situations, we pray for God to change our circumstances, but in truth, God wants to change our mind so that *we* can affect our circumstances.

I believe Satan's attack on our thoughts is a vital part

of his all-out assault on our faith, family and finances. You need to know his deceptions so you can have deliverance from his mind game.

Here is the powerful foundation scripture for this book: *"Let this mind be in you, which was also in Christ Jesus: Who, being in the form of God, thought it not robbery to be equal with God? But made himself of no reputation, and took upon him the form of a servant, and was made in the likeness of men: And being found in fashion as a man, he humbled himself, and became obedient unto death, even the death of the cross"* (Philippians 2:5-8)

It is my prayer that as a result of reading, studying and applying what is contained on these pages your thinking will be in step with the Lord.

As we begin, let me ask you to say these words out loud: "Let this mind be in me, which is also in Christ Jesus! I am who God says I am!"

This is the start of a *new you!*

— *Waylyn Hobbs, Jr.*

HOW TO MEMORIZE SCRIPTURE

The secret of becoming more like Christ is to understand and obey His Word—to hide it in our hearts for instruction and guidance.

Why should we memorize scripture? First, God commands it: *"This book of the law shall not depart out of thy mouth; but thou shalt meditate therein day and night, that thou mayest observe to do according to all that is written therein: for then thou shalt make thy way prosperous, and then thou shalt have good success"* (Joshua 1:8).

There are many other reasons as well. The Word equips us to witness (1 Peter 3:15), keeps us from iniquity (Psalm 119:9-11), builds our spiritual development (Acts 20:32) and transforms our thinking (Romans 12:1-2).

You may say, "I'm not good at memorization. How do I begin?"

Let me encourage you to put these 20 useful steps into practice:

1. Make a total commitment.

Enter into a covenant with the Lord regarding the scripture memory program on which you are about to embark. It must be a priority in your life.

2. Ask God to help you.

In prayer, let the Lord know your desire to know the scripture and ask Him to bring the words to your remembrance.

3. Set a goal.

You may want to memorize one verse a day for 52 days, or one each week during the year.

4. Choose specific "memorization" times.

I recommend spending a few minutes early each morning to repeat verses out loud. Or, you can use spare time during the day, for example while you are waiting in line, washing the dishes or even pumping gas. If you aren't in a location where you can speak, then "think" the scriptures in your mind.

5. Keep the verses with you.

Carry this book, or even copy the scriptures on 3x5 cards which you can place in your pocket or purse.

6. Speak the scripture out loud.

It is best if you memorize by speaking the scriptures verbally. You may want to try *singing* the verse—or even *praying* the scripture.

7. Focus on each word.

At first, try saying the scripture slowly, emphasizing each syllable. It will help you concentrate.

8. Read the scripture in context.

Open your Bible and look at the verses before and after the scripture you are memorizing. It will give you a clearer understanding of the meaning.

9. Try phrase-by-phrase memorization.

Instead of trying to remember a long verse all at once, break it into short phrases. Then put it all together.

10. Be precise.

Don't deviate from a word-for-word memorization. After a few days of committing a verse to memory, go back and check it for accuracy.

11. Write the scriptures.

In a spare moment during the day, write out the verse you are currently memorizing. Do this for several days.

12. Meditate on the Word.

Ponder each word of the verse and think about its meaning. If you have time, do a word study in a concordance or with a computer Bible software program.

13. Don't forget the chapter and verse.

Before quoting the scripture, say the chapter and verse out loud. For example, say: "John 3:16 – For God so loved the world...."

14. Be accountable.

If possible, invite a friend to join you in Bible memorization. By finding a time each week to quote the verses to each other it will add motivation and encouragement to your commitment.

15. Keep a log of your progress.

Either make a check mark in this book when you

have successfully memorized a scripture or enter the chapter and verse in a notebook.

16. Use word association.

Where possible, associate key words of a scripture with mental images. For example, to help remember the start of the verse,"I can do all things through Christ who strengthens me (Philippians 4:13), think of a tin can with the letter "I" painted on it. Use your imagination.

17. Use the verses in daily conversation.

When talking with a friend about spiritual matters, find an appropriate place to quote a verse—not to call attention to your memory program, but to build another in faith.

18. Build a storehouse of scripture.

After learning a new verse, go back and quote every scripture you have previously memorized. This way you reinforce what you've learned.

19. Review and repeat.

This is not a short-term project. Your objective should be to keep these scriptures fresh for the rest of your life. You should not consider a verse memorized until you have repeated it at least 100 times over several weeks!

20. Don't be limited by only 52 verses.

After you have memorized the scriptures I recommend in this book, begin to add additional verses to your memory bank. You'll be surprised how much your mind can contain!

The verses I have chosen for your memorization are meant to impact every area of your spiritual experience: salvation, prayer, the Holy Spirit, obedience, witnessing, assurance, guidance, faith, healing, provision, grace, peace and love.

The memory scriptures are a bonus feature. They were not chosen to match the chapter content, but to help you in your everyday walk with God.

It's time to begin this exciting adventure.

CHAPTER 1

IT STARTS
IN THE MIND

O n the sixth day of creation, after God spoke the world into existence, He created a masterpiece. In the image of Himself, the Almighty formed something totally unique—man.

What set this creature apart from the birds of the air or the fish of the sea was the inter-working of three forces: body, spirit and mind:

- *Our body* of flesh keeps us in touch with our surroundings—what we taste, see, smell and feel. These are our sensory perceptions.

NEW MIND! MEMORY VERSE #1

*And be not conformed
to this world: but be ye
transformed by the renewing
of your mind, that ye may
prove what is that good,
and acceptable, and
perfect, will of God.*

– ROMANS 12:2

■ Our *spirit* keeps us in touch with God. The Bible tells us: *"God is a Spirit: and they that worship him must worship him in spirit and in truth"* (John 4:24).

■ Our *mind*, or soul, keeps us in touch with ourselves—involving our thoughts and emotions.

Most people use the words "mind" and "brain" interchangeably. However our brain is not our mind—it only *houses* our mind.

In the 1970s, Dr. Roger Sperry was doing research with epileptic patients (who had one side of their brain severed to prevent seizures) and documented that the two cerebral hemispheres of the brain had distinct functions. The left, in most cases the *dominant* side, is the center of our reasoning, language, reading and writing, while the right (the less dominant) is much more involved in nonverbal processes—such as music, art and creative activities.

Dr. Perry was awarded a Nobel Prize in physiology and medicine for his "split brain" research. Yet, he was only scratching the surface of an incredible God-given gift—our mind.

Those "Happy Thoughts"

You are riding along in the car, listening to a song on

NEW MIND! MEMORY VERSE #2

For God has not given us a spirit of fear, but of power and of love and of a sound mind.

– 2 TIMOTHY 1:7

the radio—and the next thing you know, you are daydreaming about *something* or *someone* the song reminds you of.

It may have been years since you last heard the tune, but instantly you are transported back to the time or event when you first listened to the melody and words. The moment recalled may have been a young love, a vacation spot or perhaps an event while you were in college.

How does this happen? The song triggers the *endorphin* chemical in the brain, bringing back the memory.

What's amazing is that endorphins retrieve only the pleasant experiences of our past memories and actually make us feel better. These neurotransmitters, found in the brain, have pain-relieving properties similar to morphine.

THE SONG TRIGGERS THE ENDORPHIN CHEMICAL IN THE BRAIN, BRINGING BACK THE MEMORY.

Prolonged, continuous exercise contributes to an increased production and release of endorphins. The result is a sense of euphoria often called a "runner's high."

Wouldn't it be great if we could bottle this unique

NEW MIND! MEMORY VERSE #3

Peace I leave with you, my peace I give unto you: not as the world giveth, give I unto you. Let not your heart be troubled, neither let it be afraid.

– JOHN 14:27

chemical and take a sip of "happy thoughts" whenever we are feeling sad or depressed?

Well, because that's not possible, we need to learn how to renew our mind, our thinking and our outlook. The key is found by tapping into a higher source—a power unavailable through any science or medicine found on this planet. Jesus says: *"Peace I leave with you, my peace I give unto you: not as the world giveth, give I unto you. Let not your heart be troubled, neither let it be afraid"* (John 14:27).

The Gateway

While Adam possessed the three ingredients we've been discussing—body, mind and spirit—his relationship with God was centered in the *spirit* man.

When the first man and woman sinned in the Garden of Eden, it was their *spirit man* which died. The Bible tells us, *"...the spirit indeed is willing, but the flesh is weak"* (Matthew 26:41).

It is only through the death, burial and resurrection of our Lord and Savior, Jesus Christ, our spirit man can now live.

Further, it is the renewing of our mind which allows us to keep the door open to what God has placed in our heart and soul. How is this possible? Your mind acts as a gateway, giving you the ability to switch from the *flesh*

New Mind! Memory Verse #4

*Let the words of
my mouth, and the
meditation of my heart,
be acceptable in thy sight,
O Lord, my strength,
and my redeemer.*

– Psalm 19:14

man to the *spirit man.* Therefore, the renewing of the mind is the only way we can kill the *deeds* of our carnal self.

Satan's Game!

It is vital to know that when it comes to the behavior of the flesh you don't ask God to deliver you. Why? Because the Almighty has already given you the power to deliver yourself!

Read this scripture carefully: *"Therefore, brethren, we are debtors, not to the flesh, to live after the flesh. For if ye live after the flesh, ye shall die: but if ye through the Spirit do mortify the deeds of the body, ye shall live"* (Romans 8:12-13).

Who is doing the "mortifying" of the deeds of the body? You are!

When you understand this divine principle you will see why Satan has *many* reasons for attacking your mind hour after hour. It is his job to try and prevent you from having daily contact and communion with your Heavenly Father.

I trust you are beginning to realize why many of the problems you have been dealing with are not because God is mad at you. Rather, because Satan is trying to entangle you in the *mind game.*

I am convinced far too many believers in the body of Christ are allowing the devil to defeat them through this evil device.

NEW MIND! MEMORY VERSE #5

...in all these things we are more than conquerors through him that loved us.

– ROMANS 8:37

Heed these words of Peter: *"Be sober, be vigilant; because your adversary the devil, as a roaring lion, walketh about, seeking whom he may devour"* (1 Peter 5:8)

A key, but small word in this verse is— *"as."* Satan isn't an actual lion, he is *as* a lion! Many make the mistake of allowing the roaring of a toothless enemy to intimidate them—causing them to give up pursuing all God has in store.

> **MANY MAKE THE MISTAKE OF ALLOWING THE ROARING OF A TOOTHLESS ENEMY TO INTIMIDATE THEM.**

Again, Satan is playing his evil "mind game" with us.

I believe, as you continue to read this book, you will be able to differentiate between Satan, *pretending* to be a lion, and Jesus, the true Lion of Judah!

The Real You

Outside of what we receive from an omniscient, all-knowing God, the information we acquire on earth is self-knowledge—including self-concept.

It is vital to make certain your self-concept is formed by a close fellowship with the Father.

This is an area where the enemy can attack us in our

NEW MIND! MEMORY VERSE #6

I can do all things through Christ who strengthens me.

– PHILIPPIANS 4:13

Christian walk. If Satan can make me question *who* I am, then I will doubt *Whose* I am.

Thank God, I know the real me:

- I am the head and not the tail (Deuteronomy 28:13).
- I am more than a conqueror through Him who loves me (Romans 8:37).
- I can do all things through Christ who strengthens me (Philippians 4:13).

"Take No Thought"

Satan knows that the best way to infiltrate our mind is through our thoughts—to fill us with self-consuming concepts and ideas. That's why Jesus says, *"Take no thought for your life, what ye shall eat, or what ye shall drink; nor yet for your body, what ye shall put on. Is not the life more than meat, and the body than raiment?"* (Matthew 6:25).

Most Christians are stressed to the breaking point over matters God has already promised to take care of. Is it any wonder Satan takes advantage of the opportunity to further pervert and corrupt our thinking?

Of course, the devil has plenty of partners in the world of media and mass-market advertising. Instead of allowing us to be content with the clothes on our back

NEW MIND! MEMORY VERSE #7

But my God shall supply all your need according to his riches in glory by Christ Jesus.

– PHILIPPIANS 4:19

and shoes on our feet, we "just have to have" the latest designer fashions and an expensive pair of trendy sneakers.

Instead of saying, "Thank You, Lord, for being my Provider," we complain because our closet isn't overflowing with name brand apparel.

The enemy understands that if we allow material goods to consume our thinking we will spiral out of control.

Are You "Like Minded?"

A person who is self-absorbed doesn't have time to think about others.

I'm sure you have met such an individual. If you comment, "I've been having a little pain in my back lately," they seize the opportunity: "That's nothing. The doctor told me I have two slipped discs!"—then they spend two hours with their detailed litany of woes.

No matter how bad your day was, it could never compare to theirs! Even if you wanted to, you'll never out-do them in the arena of complaining.

In my years of ministry I've watched people in the body of Christ go from shouting for joy to whining over circumstances. One minute they are praising God for great victories, the next whimpering over minor setbacks.

These individuals need to get their thoughts off of

NEW MIND! MEMORY VERSE #8

Do nothing out of selfish ambition or vain conceit, but in humility consider others better than yourselves. Each of you should look not only to your own interests, but also to the interests of others.

– PHILIPPIANS 2:3-4 NIV

themselves and start living by the words of the apostle Paul: *"...then make my joy complete by being like-minded, having the same love, being one in spirit and purpose. Do nothing out of selfish ambition or vain conceit, but in humility consider others better than yourselves. Each of you should look not only to your own interests, but also to the interests of others"* (Philippians 2:2-4 NIV).

IF WE ARE SELF-CONSUMED WITH OUR PROBLEMS... HOW CAN WE BE A BLESSING TO ANYONE ELSE?

If we are self-consumed with our problems—whether health, finances, business or relationships—how can we be a blessing to anyone else?

Conformed or Transformed?

Thank God we are not called to be patterned after the world, where it is every man for himself; winner take all, loser lose all! It's far different when we live by the Word: *"And be not conformed to this world: but be ye transformed by the renewing of your mind, that ye may prove what is that good, and acceptable, and perfect, will of God"* (Romans 12:2).

There it is: A new mind—a new you!

NEW MIND! MEMORY VERSE #9

I beseech you therefore, brethren, by the mercies of God, that ye present your bodies a living sacrifice, holy, acceptable unto God, which is your reasonable service.

– ROMANS 12:1

This should be your primary objective—to have such a divine transformation *mentally* that your behavior is changed. Instead of *self* will, we begin doing *God's* will. What an amazing difference!

Too often we find ourselves coming short of this goal. We get up in the morning, saying, "Lord let this day be full of Your good, acceptable and perfect will being done in my life." Yet, that same night, we are still searching for something which even comes *close* to this measuring stick.

Your "Reasonable" Service

All of us will one day be judged according to our works and actions. John's revelation tells us what that moment will be like: *"And I saw the dead, small and great, stand before God; and the books were opened: and another book was opened, which is the book of life: and the dead were judged out of those things which were written in the books, according to their works"* (Revelation 20:12).

I'm sure you understand the importance of making sure our works pass God's test. As the apostle Paul states: *"I beseech you therefore, brethren, by the mercies of God, that ye present your bodies a living sacrifice, holy, acceptable unto God, which is your reasonable service"* (Romans 12:1).

NEW MIND! MEMORY VERSE #10

For God so loved the world, that he gave his only begotten Son, that whosoever believeth in him should not perish, but have everlasting life.

– JOHN 3:16

I've meet those who volunteer for church and community service who proudly proclaim, "Nobody sacrifices like I do."

Well, they need to think again! In God's sight it is their expected, "reasonable" service.

While growing up, I once told my mother I wanted an allowance. She asked me, "Waylyn, why do you think you deserve one?"

Being the good son I was, I began to name the entire list of how I contributed: making my bed, taking out the garbage and cutting the grass.

She smiled at me and said, "Son, that's what you are *supposed* to do—then gave me a lecture I will never forget. I thought I was going the extra mile but it was just my reasonable service!

Needed: A Radical Change in Thinking

A rich young ruler came to Jesus and asked, *"Good teacher, what must I do to inherit eternal life?"* (Luke 18:18 NIV).

"Why do you call me good?' Jesus answered. *"No one is good—except God alone. You know the commandments: 'Do not commit adultery, do not murder, do not steal, do not give false testimony, honor your father and mother'"* (Luke 18:19-20).

The man explained how he had kept the laws of the

NEW MIND! MEMORY VERSE #11

For as the heavens are higher than the earth, so are my ways higher than your ways, and my thoughts than your thoughts.

– ISAIAH 55:9

NEW MIND! NEW YOU!

Old Testament since the days of his youth.

Hearing his answer, Jesus said to him: *"You still lack one thing. Sell everything you have and give to the poor, and you will have treasure in heaven. Then come, follow me"* (v.22).

Wow! It's no wonder the man became *"very sad, because he was a man of great wealth"* (v.23).

Jesus, seeing the ruler's disappointment, continued, *"How hard it is for the rich to enter the kingdom of God! Indeed, it is easier for a camel to go through the eye of a needle than for a rich man to enter the kingdom of God"* (v.25).

Although the wealthy young man bragged about keeping the commandments, even from his youth; Jesus illustrates how this was expected. Once again, his *reasonable* service. The challenge was for the ruler to sell everything he had and give it to those less fortunate—and that required some radical thinking.

The man's problem began with his mind! In the words of Paul: *"For I say...to every man that is among you, not to think of himself more highly than he ought to think"* (Romans 12:3).

Where the Turn-Around Starts

At the dawn of each morning we need to pray, "Lord, clear my thinking of self-righteous thoughts. Let this mind be in me which was also in Christ Jesus!"

With all of our schooling and knowledge, if God didn't keep watch over our minds we wouldn't know *who* we were or *where* we were. Some individuals have all the education in the world, yet remain fools.

Right now, ask yourself, "Am I using my resources to impress people, or so God can receive His rightful glory?"

Stop occupying your thoughts with worry over what others may say about you. It is far more important to know what God thinks about your "works"—your behavior.

The turn-around begins in your mind.

CHAPTER 2

IT'S TIME FOR NEW THINKING!

Old thinking never produces new living.

There is nothing wrong with being able to reminisce or wanting to know where you came from. We don't need to fight history, but many have a habit of languishing in the past and never looking forward to the future.

My friend, when you stay locked in yesterday you'll have a very difficult time surviving today.

Sadly, the only testimony of greatness some people have is what took place twenty or thirty years ago. However, if God is the same yesterday, today and

NEW MIND! MEMORY VERSE #12

It is written; Man shall not live by bread alone, but by every word that proceedeth out of the mouth of God.

– MATTHEW 4:4

forever, since we are His people, our successes and victories should be happening *now!*

We need to have a mindset to believe, "Every day I am alive is another opportunity for me to go higher in the things of God."

The Mercy Factor

Just before the apostle Paul tells us to be *"transformed by the renewing of your mind"* (Romans 12:2), he explains how this is possible. First it requires *"the mercies of God"* (v.1).

Before we begin to worry about right *thinking*, we must realize everything we have is based on the compassion and mercy of the Almighty. It's not because we are deserving or good, rather, *God has been so good to us!*

I've met believers who are promoted in their careers and forget the source of their advancement. As I told one gentleman, "Sir, you wouldn't even have your job if it were not for the mercies of God."

I knew this was true because the executive who had the "say-so" in whether or not he was promoted, didn't particularly like the man. I continued, "Evidently, your boss wanted another individual to have your position, but

NEW MIND! MEMORY VERSE #13

And all things, whatsoever ye shall ask in prayer, believing, ye shall receive.

– MATTHEW 21:22

because God was on your side, He made a way out of no way."

I am never offended when people imply I don't deserve what I have. My success is not based on what I say or do, rather on what God has ordained for me.

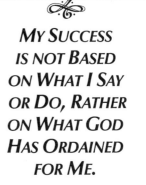

MY SUCCESS IS NOT BASED ON WHAT I SAY OR DO, RATHER ON WHAT GOD HAS ORDAINED FOR ME.

The path to a new mind is paved with God's mercies.

A Living Sacrifice

Next, we learn transformed thinking requires us to follow Paul's counsel and *"present your bodies a living sacrifice"* (v.1).

In Old Testament times, in order to have atonement for sin, people were required to come before the High Priest and offer up a sacrifice. Through Moses, God declared, *"And the priest shall make an atonement for all the congregation of the children of Israel, and it shall be forgiven them; for it is ignorance: and they shall bring their offering, a sacrifice made by fire unto the Lord, and their sin offering before the Lord, for their ignorance"* (Numbers 15:25).

NEW MIND! MEMORY VERSE #14

Be careful for nothing; but in every thing by prayer and supplication with thanksgiving let your requests be made known unto God. And the peace of God, which passeth all understanding, shall keep your hearts and minds through Christ Jesus.

– PHILIPPIANS 4:6-7

When God's Son, Jesus, came to earth and died on the cross for our sin, everything changed. No longer does our Father require *dead* offerings, He wants *living* sacrifices—for you and me to present ourselves to the Lord.

As *"lively stones,* [we] *are built up a spiritual house, an holy priesthood, to offer up spiritual sacrifices, acceptable to God by Jesus Christ"* (1 Peter 2:5).

Don't Hesitate to Ask

There are people who believe in order to prove how deep they are in God and how profound their relationship is, they must suffer. You don't need to arrive at church looking like you've barely survived a major battle with Satan. No. As a child of God you represent *life*, and *abundance*, not death!

God's Word says, *"Beloved, I wish above all things that thou mayest prosper and be in health, even as thy soul prospereth"* (3 John 1:2).

I am convinced many today are poor because they suffer from mental poverty.

Satan would love you to believe your *lack* is a sign of commitment, but remember, the devil is a liar. Look closely at the words Jesus taught us to pray: *"Give us this*

NEW MIND! MEMORY VERSE #15

Whoever has my commands and obeys them, he is the one who loves me. He who loves me will be loved by my Father, and I too will love him and show myself to him.

– JOHN 14:21 NIV

day our daily bread" (Matthew 6:11).

If God wanted us to starve, why would His Son tell us to ask for our daily sustenance?

Your day is not designed as a time of begging, rather of anticipation—being ready to receive what God has promised. You don't need to plead for something you already have. Simply request it!

YOU DON'T NEED TO PLEAD FOR SOMETHING YOU ALREADY HAVE. SIMPLY REQUEST IT!

Jesus says, *"Ask, and it shall be given you; seek, and ye shall find; knock, and it shall be opened unto you"* (Matthew 7:7 KJV).

- If you have a problem asking, close your mouth.
- If you have a problem seeking, shut your eyes.
- If you have a problem knocking, put your hands behind your back.

However, don't get envious or upset with the man or woman who takes God at His Word and boldly requests everything the Lord has in store for them.

NEW MIND! MEMORY VERSE #16

Follow me, and I will make you fishers of men.

– MATTHEW 4:19

Right is Right!

If you want to know what a person is made of, start by finding out what they believe in. It's impossible to have a solid moral foundation without a bedrock of strong conviction and belief. The words I was taught as a child still ring true: "If you don't stand for something, you will fall for anything."

Unfortunately, many young people have not been raised to understand *right is right* and *wrong is wrong.* Instead, they have been brainwashed by a generation who practice situational ethics—"Just say whatever makes you look good and keeps you out of trouble for the present situation."

I can remember the time when even those who didn't attend church had enough intelligence to believe there was a God and reverenced a house of worship.

Whose Reality?

I shudder to think what will become of children who are being raised to believe in *nothing.* They spend thousands of hours absorbed in so-called "virtual reality"— their attention glued to the screen of the latest video game.

For example, what can we expect of a youngster who wastes his time playing a game about auto theft, spending countless hours stealing cars in order to progress to the next level?

A young person does not always have the knowledge or experience to understand if what they do in a game is duplicated in the real world they will suffer great consequences.

In a game, when you shoot somebody, you just press "reset" and they bounce back to life. In reality, if you kill a person, it's over! There are no second chances.

Oh, how I pray we can turn these young minds around so they will know the joy of the Lord before it is too late.

Don't Live Among the Dead

If you desire a "right mind" you must stay in the right environment. Jesus once found Himself confronted by a man who was possessed by devils and was so deranged he made his home in the graveyard. Because his mind was gone, he chose the wrong environment.

"What is your name?" asked Jesus.

The man answered, *"Legion: because many devils were entered into him"* (Luke 8:30).

Jesus cast the demons out of the tormented man and the people flocked to see what had taken place. They *"found the man, out of whom the devils were departed, sitting at the feet of Jesus, clothed, and in his right mind"* (Luke 8:35).

How can we expect a renewed mind if we are living and playing among the dead things of our world?

The Lord says, *"Consider your ways. Ye have sown much, and bring in little; ye eat, but ye have not enough; ye drink, but ye are not filled with drink; ye clothe you, but there is none warm; and he that earneth wages earneth wages to put it into a bag with holes"* (Haggai 1:5-6).

We must know our surroundings. Why waste money on temporary pleasures when you could be investing in your future? Why consume your thoughts on Satan's distractions when God offers you an abundant life?

The choice is yours.

CHAPTER 3

THE GREAT TRANSFORMATION

The "new you" which results from a transformed mind is not a carbon copy of another person—it is God's way of making you totally unique.

Some who suffer from a poor self-image rush to a plastic surgeon and say "I need an extreme make-over!"

Think how much time, money and pain they would save if they simply asked the Lord to radically change them, starting with their mind. Authentic beauty radiates from what is on the inside and shows on your face. It's a make-over only Almighty God can perform.

It's time to stop saying, "I want to be like him" or "I

NEW MIND! MEMORY VERSE #17

*But ye shall receive
power, after that the Holy
Ghost is come upon you:
and ye shall be witnesses
unto me both in Jerusalem,
and in all Judaea, and
in Samaria, and unto
the uttermost part
of the earth.*

– ACTS 1:8

wish I could look like her." Instead, ask the Lord, "Make me who *You* want me to be."

The Real You

As a minister, I have watched new converts attempt to imitate seasoned saints—believing it's the only way other Christians are going to accept them. They think, "If I don't shout or raise my hands like Sister Sue, I'm not praising God."

That's foolishness! Since the Lord knows your heart, it is immaterial what others think of your style of worship. Yes, we are all saved the same glorious way, but there are differences in how we praise our Heavenly Father.

When God renews your mind, He addresses *your* personal situation, not that of someone else. No matter how hard I try, I can never be you, and you can never be me. We are distinct individuals with our own personalities.

Just as we were created with one-of-a-kind physical characteristics, the Lord desires an individual relationship with each of His children.

"Here Am I"

If you want a transformed mind, admit your faults and allow God to begin a new work in you. This was Isaiah's

New Mind! Memory Verse #18

*For I am not ashamed
of the gospel of Christ: for
it is the power of God unto
salvation to every one
that believeth.*

– Romans 1:16

NEW MIND! NEW YOU!

key to being used mightily by the Lord.

When King Uzziah died, Isaiah had a vision. He writes, *"I saw also the Lord sitting upon a throne, high and lifted up, and his train filled the temple"* (Isaiah 6:1).

This was in total contrast to how he viewed his own life. He said to himself, *"Woe is me! for I am undone; because I am a man of unclean lips, and I dwell in the midst of a people of unclean lips: for mine eyes have seen the King, the Lord of hosts"* (v.5).

HE DIDN'T BLAME HIS PROBLEMS ON HIS UPBRINGING OR THE PEOPLE WITH WHOM HE ASSOCIATED.

He didn't blame his problems on his upbringing or the people with whom he associated. Instead, Isaiah took full responsibility for his personal shortcomings and failures, admitting his lips were "unclean."

The Lord, searching the land for the person to replace King Uzziah as the leader of the Israelites, saw in Isaiah a man with the right qualities. No, he wasn't perfect, yet he was willing to be used of the Lord.

Next, Isaiah *"heard the voice of the Lord, saying, Whom shall I send, and who will go for us? Then said I, Here am I; send me"* (v.6).

With a new mind, you are ready to serve!

NEW MIND! MEMORY VERSE #19

Go ye therefore, and teach all nations, baptizing them in the name of the Father, and of the Son, and of the Holy Ghost.

– MATTHEW 28:19

Shifting the Blame

The burdens of life are lifted when you are totally honest and transparent in your approach to God. Two biblical characters, Adam and David, illustrate this point.

When Adam sinned in the Garden of Eden by eating of the forbidden tree, the Creator looked for him in the cool of the day and asked, *"Where art thou?"* (Genesis 3:9).

Overcome by guilt, Adam responded, "I'm hiding here because I am naked and afraid."

God then asked this penetrating question, "Who told you that you were naked?"

The answer was obvious. Adam was the cause of the problem and was riddled with shame. Yet, he attempted to make excuses and shift the blame.

Instead of readily admitting his faults, Adam said, *"The woman whom thou gavest to be with me, she gave me of the tree, and I did eat"* (v.12).

The Confession

Contrast this with how David responded to his failures.

One evening, as David walked onto the roof of his house, he noticed a beautiful woman on a rooftop below

NEW MIND! MEMORY VERSE #20

For the wages of sin is death; but the gift of God is eternal life through Jesus Christ our Lord.

– ROMANS 6:23

taking a bath. He learned her name was Bathsheba, the wife of Uriah, a soldier who was off fighting with David's army (1 Samuel 11).

When David discovered the woman was married, he should have immediately controlled his desire. However, he had an affair with Bathsheba, then tried to conceal his sin. When that failed, he arranged for Uriah to be conveniently killed in battle so he could pursue his lust.

David was convicted and knew it was impossible to hide from God. So instead of blaming the mistake on Bathsheba or making excuses to the Lord (as did Adam), he confessed and begged for forgiveness, pleading, *"Have mercy upon me, O God, according to thy lovingkindness: according unto the multitude of thy tender mercies blot out my transgressions. Wash me thoroughly from mine iniquity, and cleanse me from my sin. For I acknowledge my transgressions: and my sin is ever before me"* (Psalm 51:1-3).

To make his confession even clearer to the Lord, David admits, *"Against thee, thee only, have I sinned, and done this evil in thy sight"* (v.4).

Finally, David prayed, *"Create in me a clean heart, O God; and renew a right spirit within me. Cast me not away from thy presence; and take not thy holy spirit from me. Restore unto me the joy of thy salvation"* (vv.10-12).

NEW MIND! MEMORY VERSE #21

For by grace are ye saved through faith; and that not of yourselves: it is the gift of God: Not of works, lest any man should boast.

– EPHESIANS 2:8-9

The Lord not only forgave David, He restored him to a position of leadership and said, *"I have found David... a man after mine own heart"* (Acts 13:22).

"It's All My Fault"

If you are entrapped by temptation and make a horrible mistake, how will you react? Will you look for a scapegoat and say, "The devil made me do it!"? I certainly hope not.

"LORD FORGIVE ME. I AM ASKING YOU TO WASH ME AND MAKE ME WHITER THAN SNOW.

Be man or woman enough to admit, "God, I messed up—it's all my fault." Then take the next step and pray, "Lord forgive me. I am asking You to wash me and make me whiter than snow."

An Offering of Tears

I love reading the account of the woman who came to Jesus in the middle of the day. She was a lowly prostitute, but when she heard Jesus was in a particular house, she bravely broke through the doors, fell before Him, *"and began to wash his feet with tears, and did*

NEW MIND! MEMORY VERSE #22

*These things have I
written unto you that
believe on the name of
the Son of God; that ye may
know that ye have eternal
life, and that ye may
believe on the name
of the Son of God.*

– 1 JOHN 5:13

wipe them with the hairs of her head, and kissed his feet, and anointed them with the ointment"(Luke 7:38).

Here was a woman who certainly had no hymn to sing or scripture to read. She was expressing her innermost thoughts, "Jesus, the only thing I have to offer is who I am. My tears are just an expression of what I am feeling on the inside. Lord, I give You my heart."

Jesus said to the people who had gathered, *"Her sins, which are many, are forgiven; for she loved much"* (Luke 7:47).

> *WE ARE TO COME BEFORE THE FATHER JUST AS WE ARE—WITH ALL OF OUR PERSONAL BAGGAGE.*

The Bible tells us those who worship Him, are to do so *"in spirit and in truth"* (John 4:24). In other words, we are to come before the Father just as we are—with all of our personal baggage.

A New Me!

Personally, there was a time in my life when nothing seemed to work. All of my plans miserably failed and my dreams were dashed.

Then one day I came to Jesus and gave Him my life.

He picked me up, turned me around and placed my feet on solid ground. Then as I began to treasure His Word in my heart, He gave me a brand new mind—and a new attitude.

This is why I can tell the Lord:

- "I didn't come to praise You for who I am, but for who You are."
- "I didn't come to praise you for what I did, but for what You did."
- I didn't come to praise you for where I came from, but for where You are taking me."

Like David, I can say, *"Thou hast turned...my mourning into dancing"* (Psalm 30:11). He has changed my tears into laughter.

I received a double portion. Not only do I have a new mind—I have a new *me!* Things that once burdened my spirit and laid me low have vanished like a vapor. What I worried about no longer seems important. Now all I can think of are the blessings the Lord is waiting to pour out on me tomorrow.

Oh, what a transformation took place when I met Jesus:

- He's my doctor in the sickroom.
- He's my lawyer in the courtroom.
- He's my bread when I am hungry.
- He's my water when I am thirsty.

I can't stop praising His Holy Name. He puts joy in my heart, praise in my mouth and fire in my soul!

CHAPTER 4

THE GUILT TRIP

I remember talking with a young man who wanted to get his life together. "What's holding you back?" I wanted to know.

"Well, " he began, "I did something in my past I'm afraid will catch up with me."

On further questioning, I learned he had a minor traffic infraction several months earlier, but at the time he was to appear in court, he didn't have the money to pay his fine. Since he failed to show up, he just knew there was a warrant out for his arrest.

The young man's anxiety over being apprehended by the law was so great he didn't even want to leave his house—and he stopped going to work and school.

NEW MIND! MEMORY VERSE #23

If any of you lacks wisdom, he should ask God, who gives generously to all without finding fault, and it will be given to him.

– JAMES 1:5 NIV

Finally, I was able to convince him to call the traffic court to set up a date for another hearing. "I'll even go with you," I offered.

He did as I suggested, and I kept my end of the bargain. After appearing before the judge and paying a fine of $125, the problem was resolved.

You're Not Alone

Think of it! The guilt of his past blinded his reasoning. The fear of what *might* happen must be replaced by the reality of what *will* happen if we do what is right.

Don't allow *anything*, no matter how great or small, to keep you trapped in the past. You must confront it, admit it, and resolve it!

We are not facing life's problems alone, God reassures us, *"When thou passest through the waters, I will be with thee: and through the rivers, they shall not overflow thee: when thou walkest through the fire, thou shalt not be burned, neither shall the flame kindle upon thee"* (Isaiah 43:2).

> **DON'T ALLOW ANYTHING, NO MATTER HOW GREAT OR SMALL, TO KEEP YOU TRAPPED IN THE PAST.**

NEW MIND! MEMORY VERSE #24

*Trust in the Lord
with all thine heart;
and lean not unto thine
own understanding. In all
thy ways acknowledge
him, and he shall
direct thy paths.*

– PROVERBS 3:5-6

The Wrong Trip

Satan never stops playing his "mind games," trying to manipulate your thoughts and actions. In order to distract you from fulfilling God's purpose in your life, he encourages people to send you on a guilt trip.

How does this happen? Often, the devil uses family and friends to subtly govern your actions—by instilling a sense of self-shame if you fail to help them.

As a result, you:

- Spend time and resources trying to help those you are not obligated to in any way.
- Try to assist people who are not attempting to help themselves.
- Lend money to a person who has no intention of paying you back—squandering it on anything but the reason they said it was needed.

Please don't get me wrong; we should support those in need, but *where* we sow is just as important as sowing. Jesus says, *"Give not that which is holy unto the dogs, neither cast ye your pearls before swine, lest they*

NEW MIND! MEMORY VERSE #25

*The Lord is good, a
stronghold in the day of
trouble; and he knoweth
them that trust him.*

– *NAHUM 1:7*

trample them under their feet, and turn again and rend you" (Matthew 7:6).

Pigs have no idea of the value of pearls, so they *walk* all over them! We, as humans, know better. So don't get upset with a friend because you loaned him your car and he brought it back out of gas—with five parking tickets on the windshield!

Ask yourself, "Was it really God's will for me to loan my vehicle, or was I hoodwinked by his story?"

It is this same thinking which causes people to give to fake charities and other scams. Does the man standing on a corner with a sign that reads, "Will work for food," really want a job, or simply a handout for more alcohol?

Stand Your Ground

Guilt also finds its way into our home.

For example, as a Christian parent, you have an obligation to make decisions based on what is right for your children—even if they vehemently disagree. It's not uncommon for a teen to say,

AS A CHRISTIAN PARENT, YOU HAVE AN OBLIGATION TO MAKE DECISIONS ON WHAT IS RIGHT FOR YOUR CHILD.

NEW MIND! MEMORY VERSE #26

I am crucified with Christ: nevertheless I live; yet not I, but Christ liveth in me: and the life which I now live in the flesh I live by the faith of the Son of God, who loved me, and gave himself for me.

– GALATIANS 2:20

"Mom, I'm going to a party tonight and won't be home till about two o'clock in the morning,"

You answer firmly. "Son, you know your weekend curfew. I expect you here by 11 o'clock sharp!"

He stomps his feet and complains, "Well, everybody else's parents are letting their kids go!"

Once again, a bucket of guilt has been poured all over you, but remain firm and stand your ground. Failure to "train up a child in the way he should go" will have a rippling negative effect on the remainder of his life.

I tell my own children, "You may be mad at me today, but you'll thank me tomorrow."

AS LONG AS WE ALLOW SATAN TO CONTROL OUR THINKING THROUGH GUILT, WE WILL NEVER STAY ON THE ROAD TO GODLY SUCCESS.

As long as we allow Satan to control our thinking through guilt, we will never stay on the road to Godly success.

"I Felt Obligated"

The guilt problem arrives in many forms.

NEW MIND! MEMORY VERSE #27

*A time is coming
and has now come when
the true worshipers will
worship the Father in spirit
and truth, for they are
the kind of worshipers
the Father seeks.*

– John 4:23 NIV

A marriage can suffer because a couple allows a relative they haven't seen in years to move into their home.

"I felt obligated to take him in," a husband told me, "but the peace in our household has flown out the window!"

Of course, we should always be compassionate to those in need, yet we must seek the Lord first and pray for His direction. The Bible says, *"Beloved, let us love one another: for love is God: and every one that loveth is born of God, and knoweth God"* (1 John 4:7-12). At the same time we are to pray for the Lord's wisdom.

We all have family members who struggle in many areas, yet we know if they would just turn their life over to Christ, things would change dramatically. If winning them to the Lord is our objective, we should be more than willing to open our hearts.

Satan would rather make us feel obligated to help our family members through guilt than through the Word of God. The devil wants our good intentions to turn into disaster.

God's Family

Study scripture and learn what *He* desires. Jesus

NEW MIND! MEMORY VERSE #28

Let your conversation be without covetousness; and be content with such things as ye have: for he hath said, I will never leave thee, nor forsake thee.

– HEBREWS 13:5

declared, *"For whosoever shall do the will of my Father, which is in heaven, the same is my brother, and sister, and mother"* (Matthew 12:50).

Yes, blood is thicker than water, but thank God, everyone who has been washed in the blood of the Lamb, is now my brother and sister.

When a relative criticizes, "You look out for your church friends more than me," let them know that in Christ, we are *all* family. As the Bible tells us, *"For both he that sanctifieth and they who are sanctified are all of one: for which cause he is not ashamed to call them brethren."* (Hebrews 2:11).

If the Lord has placed you in a position to bless others, make sure your orders come from above.

"No Condemnation"

Thank God, we do not need to live under a cloud of guilt. The apostle Paul counsels, *"There is therefore now no condemnation to them which are in Christ Jesus, who walk not after the flesh, but after the Spirit"* (Romans 8:1).

See Satan's schemes for what they truly are. Guilt which originates because of the actions of others is not worth your worry—ask the Lord to erase it from your thought process.

It's only your personal guilt of sin that must be dealt with, and it is cleansed the moment you ask Christ to become your Lord and Savior.

Satan continues to play his games, but remember, you are on the winning side!

CHAPTER 5

THE ART OF INTIMIDATION

As a teenager in school we played a game call "Flinch."

The object was to act like you were going to hit your opponent. If he moved or *flinched* than you were allowed to give him a strong punch in the arm.

It was a mind game—and to insure an easy win all you had to do was just clench your fist and aim your punch close enough to your opponent's arm, without actually striking him. This would cause the persons natural defenses to kick in, and they would automatically flinch.

It's sad to say, but many are playing the same game in

NEW MIND! MEMORY VERSE #29

Thou wilt keep him in perfect peace, whose mind is stayed on thee: because he trusteth in thee.

– ISAIAH 26:3

NEW MIND! NEW YOU!

adulthood, but this time with Satan. They go through a routine of pretending they have a powerful prayer life, speaking phrases they heard someone say in church and claiming victory over their family and finances—all the while hoping Satan will flinch!

The Fear Factor

Intimidation takes on many forms. Examine military history and you will see how armies have been victorious simply by instilling fear and panic in the enemy camp through false rumors and misinformation.

In World War II, when the Allied forces were ready to invade the beaches of Normandy, they used a ploy to confuse Hitler's army. Dummy parachuters were dropped away from the point of invasion so the enemy would think the battle would occur in another location. It led to a major victory for the Allies.

Today, terrorist organizations not only use suicide bombers, they use the *threat* of bombs to intimidate nations. If fear will keep people from riding in buses, eating in restaurants and disrupting their daily lives, the terrorists have achieved their goal.

We see the same phenomena in sports. For example, if a basketball team has made up its mind their opponent

85

NEW MIND! MEMORY VERSE #30

But the fruit of the Spirit is love, joy, peace, patience, kindness, goodness, faithfulness, gentleness and self-control. Against such things there is no law.

– GALATIANS 5:22-23

is faster and more skillful, the game is lost before it is ever played.

Conditioned for Failure?

Psychologists describe a condition called "learned helplessness." In one study, Dr. Martin Seligman, professor of psychology at the University of Pennsylvania, placed two dogs in separate boxes—with a low fence they could jump over if they wished.

The first dog had been "conditioned" by placing it in a restraining device and repeatedly given a harmless electrical shock. The second dog had no conditioning.

When both animals were later administered the same shock, the second dog jumped over the fence while the first "conditioned" dog, although unrestrained, just laid there pathetically.

Evidently, he had concluded trying to escape was futile—he had learned to be helpless!

This is why we should be slow to judge those who don't seem to take advantage of opportunities to change their lifestyles. Their minds have been programmed by the environment in which they have been raised.

When people experience painful events over which they have no control, they become helpless. Then, if intimidation is piled on top of their problems, life can

NEW MIND! MEMORY VERSE #31

*But as many as received
him, to them gave he power
to become the sons of God,
even to them that believe
on his name.*

– *JOHN 1:12*

seem dismal and hopeless.

There's an Answer

Circumstances often present situations where we can't see our way out. Because of fear, we find ourselves remembering the worst scenarios we have ever heard—accounts of people in similar conditions and their horrific outcomes. So, defeated, we give up without a fight!

THANK GOD, THERE IS A SOLUTION TO DESPAIR.

Thank God, there is a solution to despair. What we need to remember is, *"For God hath not given us the spirit of fear; but of power, and of love, and of a sound mind"* (2 Timothy 1:7).

A Life-Changing Vision

At the age of fourteen, the Lord called me into the ministry. Jesus appeared to me in a vision—I remember it as if it was yesterday.

I was walking in what appeared to be a metropolitan area. (I mention this because I grew up in the suburbs and really didn't know much about the inner city.) As I

NEW MIND! MEMORY VERSE #32

And the Word was made flesh, and dwelt among us, (and we beheld his glory, the glory as of the only begotten of the Father,) full of grace and truth.

– JOHN 1:14

continued, Jesus came near, asking me to tell the people they could be free.

In the vision, the Lord pointed to a field where throngs were fighting, shooting drugs—indulging in all kind of vices. Then I saw two men standing in front of a gate that led to the field. In their hands were bats and chains; it was their job to stand guard and prevent the people from escaping. I panicked, and as soon as Jesus left the scene, I started running, trying to find a way to get out of the city and back to the suburbs.

As the vision continued, I asked a homeless man sitting on the curb. "How do I get back to my home? I am lost."

When the indigent man looked up at me, it was the beautiful face of Jesus! He answered, "Go and free my people!"

Immediately, I did what the Lord asked—going back into the middle of the crowd, declaring, "Jesus said you can be totally free!"

They began to run out of the gate and the guards started to attack me with their bats and chains. Yet amazingly, the more they struck me, the less pain I felt. Next I heard the voice of Jesus say, "Do My will and I will protect you from the enemy."

When the vision was over I realized Jesus wanted me

NEW MIND! MEMORY VERSE #33

The Lord is faithful, and he will strengthen and protect you from the evil one.

– 2 THESSALONIANS 3:3 NIV

to do something I had no prior intention of ever doing—yet now, no threats could keep me from this assignment.

An Intense Struggle

I was 30 years of age when God called me to become a pastor. The church was 65 years old with a membership of less than 30 people.

When the Lord began to pour out His blessing and people began to fill the sanctuary, I saw the art of intimidation first-hand. Some of the original members felt they were being replaced—so they tried everything in their power to make the new members feel unwelcomed.

I could see why they were threatened. Because of the neighborhood in which we were located, many of the new believers were former drug addicts and gang members—and their attire was not always what the "old timers" thought was appropriate for a house of worship.

As pastor, however, I felt strongly our mission was to bring people in, not to chase them away.

The struggle became intense, with church members intimidating me to either do things their way, or hit the highway! Here I was, involved in something I had never

NEW MIND! MEMORY VERSE #34

Know ye not that ye are the temple of God, and that the Spirit of God dwelleth in you?

– 1 CORINTHIANS 3:16

planned—yet I was following the Father's vision for my life.

Thank God, I didn't listen to the negative voices. The Lord brought unity and harmony among believers, and the church has grown to over 2000 members. Together, we are touching the lives of thousands in our community.

The Completed Story

Don't allow anyone to deter you! There is an unseen hand guiding your steps: *"Looking unto Jesus the author and finisher of our faith; who for the joy that was set before him endured the cross, despising the shame, and is set down at the right hand of the throne of God"* (Hebrews 12:2).

People can read the first chapters of your life, but only Jesus will write the ending! Praise God, He is both the author and *finisher* of our journey of faith.

CHAPTER 6

IT'S NOT AN ILLUSION

Have you ever seen a magician make a table "float," or watched as he sawed a woman in half?

What you actually witnessed was an illusion—what the dictionary defines as (1) a mistaken idea or (2) a misleading visual image. In other words, you saw something that didn't really happen!

The mind has a great influence over your senses and can actually override your eyes.

Without realizing it, we can find ourselves in problems or conflicts because of things we thought we saw or heard. Countless friendships, relationships, businesses and churches have been devastated by illusions.

NEW MIND! MEMORY VERSE #35

*God is able to make
all grace abound toward
you; that ye, always having
all sufficiency in all things,
may abound to every
good work.*

– 2 CORINTHIANS 9:8

Two Different Views

I once was asked to counsel with two women in the church who were at odds with each other. The deacons had tried unsuccessfully to have them come and reason together, now they were asking me to intervene.

When I inquired, "What is the cause of this dissension between you two?" one woman began by telling me, "A few Sundays ago I said 'Hello' and she completely ignored me and just walked away."

The woman who was charged with being rude remembered it totally differently.

On further questioning, I learned on that particular Sunday, the accused woman had a minor car accident on the way to church—and was shaken up. At the meeting she said, "I apologize if I didn't speak to you. There was so much on my mind, I don't think I even heard you."

The sister who originally brought the charge had tears in her eyes and began to confess, "That morning, the Holy Spirit told me, for some reason, to go and comfort you. And when I thought you ignored me, I became angry and offended."

God touched their hearts and both asked forgiveness. The issue was history.

NEW MIND! MEMORY VERSE #36

The Lord is my rock, and my fortress, and my deliverer; my God, my strength, in whom I will trust; my buckler, and the horn of my salvation, and my high tower.

– PSALM 18:2

By acting on what she *thought* she saw, the woman missed a chance to be a blessing to the sister in her time of distress.

Listen to Your Spirit

Don't be misguided by the devils illusions which fool your senses and cause you to believe a lie. The next time Satan tries to bring division in a relationship, give the other person the benefit of the doubt.

Most important, learn to let your spirit speak to your mind. When the enemy attempts to turn your focus on divisive problems, say, "Mind, you had better listen to what God has spoken to my spirit. I claim victory, not defeat."

> DON'T BE MISGUIDED BY THE DEVIL'S ILLUSIONS WHICH FOOL YOUR SENSES AND CAUSE YOU TO BELIEVE A LIE.

From the beginning, the Bible tells us, *"Now the serpent was more subtle than any beast of the field which the Lord God had made"* (Genesis 3:1).

He sowed seeds of doubt in Eve: "Did God really say you must not eat from the tree in the garden? Surely you will not die."

NEW MIND! MEMORY VERSE #37

Thou wilt keep him in perfect peace, whose mind is stayed on thee: because he trusteth in thee.

– ISAIAH 26:3

As long as the devil can make you question God's Word, he knows you will then relay this to your senses and make the wrong choice. This is evident in the actions of Eve. Scripture records, *"And when the woman saw that the tree was good for food, and that it was pleasant to the eyes, and a tree to be desired to make one wise, she took of the fruit thereof, and did eat, and gave also unto her husband with her; and he did eat"* (v.6).

In the words of an old saying, "Everything that looks good *to* you isn't good *for* you."

Why Unnecessary Stress?

Today, instead of standing firm on the Word, many are inclined to chase the illusions Satan dangles before them. As a result, they waver and take their eyes off God's purpose and plan and rely on their own senses, falling prey to Satan's tricks.

My friend, don't drive yourself crazy and become mentally troubled over things God promises He will take care of. Jesus assures you, *"Take no thought for your life, what ye shall eat, or what ye shall drink; nor yet for your body, what ye shall put on. Is not life more than meat, and the body than raiment? Behold the fowls of the air: for they sow not, neither do they reap, nor gather into*

NEW MIND! MEMORY VERSE #38

*Verily, verily, I say
unto you, He that heareth
my word, and believeth on
him that sent me, hath
everlasting life, and shall not
come into condemnation;
but is passed from
death unto life.*

– JOHN 5:24

barns; yet your heavenly Father feedeth them. Are ye not much better than they?" (Matthew 6:25-26).

If you find yourself feeling stressed over what God promises to take care of, you are following the enemy's deception.

Take time to say, "Satan, you are a liar and a deceiver! My God will supply all of my needs according to His riches in heaven!"

He will! Jesus declares, *"But seek ye first the kingdom of God, and his righteousness; and all these things shall be added unto you"* (v.33).

Your Inheritance

The reason I urge you to memorize scripture is when the Word is settled in your mind and heart, it will shatter any false illusion Satan would have you believe.

WHEN THE WORD IS SETTLED IN YOUR MIND AND HEART, IT WILL SHATTER ANY FALSE ILLUSION SATAN WOULD HAVE YOU BELIEVE.

Remember, we are not conformed, or "patterned after" the principles of this world. Instead, through Christ our Lord, *"we have obtained an inheritance, being*

NEW MIND! MEMORY VERSE #39

God is our refuge and strength, a very present help in trouble.

– PSALM 46:1

predestinated according to the purpose of him who worketh all things after the counsel of his own will" (Ephesians 1:11).

Hallucinations!

We are often afraid of the dark because when we can't see anything physically, our imagination goes into overdrive—creating the "apparent perception" of sights and sounds which don't really exist.

In essence, we are *hallucinating!*

Where do these perceptions originate? They spring from things we have heard, seen, or read about in the past.

Before children start watching scary movies, or listening to people talk about horror stories, they have no preconceived fear of the dark. After such input, however, their mind has enough ammunition to arouse all kinds of fear.

If you allow Satan to bombard your thoughts with distortions you will eventually try to "hallucinate" your way out of trouble. As Christians, however, we walk by faith, not by sight. Our belief is real and tangible—with substance and evidence. As the Bible says, *"Now faith is the substance of things hoped for, the evidence of things not seen"* (Hebrews 11:1).

NEW MIND! MEMORY VERSE #40

*Be still, and know that
I am God: I will be exalted
among the heathen, I will
be exalted in the earth.*

– PSALM 46:10

Not Ashamed

Far too often, well-meaning believers allow their minds to be cluttered with thoughts which are totally out of the will of the Father. This is the result of acting on imaginations rather than claiming God's promises by faith.

We need to pray the words of Isaiah: *"For the Lord God will help me; therefore shall I not be confounded: therefore have I set my face like a flint, and I know that I shall not be ashamed"* (Isaiah 50:7).

Headed for a Fall?

As a child I always loved horses. However, it wasn't until I was a young adult with a job that I began taking riding lessons at a local stable. I did this for a long period until my career started taking up too much of my time.

I stopped horseback riding altogether for about eight years, when suddenly I had the itch to try it again.

I started by retaking lessons, then once I got back into the feel of things, I actually bought a horse. It was my dream come true!

One day at the stable I saw an excellent rider—much better than me—fall from her mount. From that time forward, every time I got into the saddle, the only thing I could think of was falling! Even when I was grooming my horse, it preyed on my mind. After all, if an experienced rider could take a tumble, I knew it was just a matter of time until I was next.

The situation became noticeable to my instructor and we discussed the matter. He said, "You're a good rider, but you need to get this idea of falling out of your mind."

I was so wrapped up in the possibility of something which had never happened to me, I was missing out on the joys of why I loved horseback riding.

WE MUST NOT ALLOW WHAT HAPPENS TO OTHERS INFLICT DOUBT AND FEAR IN OUR MIND AND EMOTIONS.

It took a while, but I finally was able to overcome my fear by focusing on the reason I wanted to ride in the first place—the peace and quiet of riding on an open trail.

It's Not the End

We must not allow what happens to others inflict doubt and fear in our mind and emotions. The ultimate outcome is governed by the will of God and our faith in Him.

As Jesus said concerning Lazarus, *"This sickness is not unto death"* (John 11:4)—even though it sure seems like it sometimes.

The loss of a job is not the end of your career, but you'd think it was if you listened to the negative voices of those around you. Likewise, the snag in your relationship, isn't the death-knell of your marriage—regardless of what the nay-sayers predict.

Instead of listening to the prophets of doom, take it to the Lord in prayer. As Jesus tells us, *"But when you pray, go into your room, close the door and pray to your Father, who is unseen. Then your Father, who sees what is done in secret, will reward you"* (Matthew 6:6 NIV).

Get away from the crowd and lock out the pessimism causing you to lose focus. This is the time to say a permanent "farewell" to the world's illusions and experience the reality of God's abundant life.

CHAPTER 7

THE KEYS TO MIND RENEWAL

Can you remember learning to drive a car? Every ounce of concentration you could muster was applied to the task—making sure you were steering in the right direction, watching your speed and trying not to press the brake pedal down too hard when it came time to stop.

Now we do those things subconsciously. We drive and multi-task at the same time, drinking coffee, talking on our cell phone and keeping the kids quiet in the back seat.

Our thought process is amazing. Constantly, our intentional thinking is overwritten by our subconscious

NEW MIND! MEMORY VERSE #41

For we have not an high priest which cannot be touched with the feeling of our infirmities; but was in all points tempted like as we are, yet without sin. Let us therefore come boldly unto the throne of grace, that we may obtain mercy, and find grace to help in time of need.

– Hebrews 4:15-16

mind. For example, if you are riding in the passenger seat of the car and it looks like the driver is about to hit the back of the vehicle ahead, you start applying an imaginary brake.

What causes this automatic reaction? The mental activity just below your level of awareness kicks in and causes you to repeat what you were taught years before, when you first learned to drive.

Following a Pattern

One morning, on the way to the office, I was at a traffic light that takes forever to change. I thought, "If I would drive just one more block over when leaving my house, I could avoid this light altogether."

The next morning, I climbed into my car and instinctively followed the exact same path—right back to the traffic light from hell! Once more, I reminded myself, "The next time I am going to take a new route."

This happened a couple more times until I actually remembered my own advice. Why? Because subconsciously I was following a pattern which had been etched into my psyche.

Living Out the Lyrics

We need to fiercely guard what we allow to enter into

NEW MIND! MEMORY VERSE #42

Behold, I stand at the door, and knock: if any man hear my voice, and open the door, I will come in to him, and will sup with him, and he with me.

– REVELATION 3:20

our thought process. Otherwise, certain thoughts will take residence in the dark corners of our thinking and began to infect us like a virus.

In the name of corporate profits, record company executives turn deaf ears to the lyrics of gangster rap artists—who babble on and on about selling drugs, abusing women and gunning down enemies.

Those same musicians, because they are making millions, no longer live in the "hood," rather, they live in luxurious gated communities. But what about the impressionable young people who listen to these CDs? They are shooting each other in the streets—living out the lyrics.

Parents who wonder why their little princess wants to dress like a woman of the night, only need look at music video channels—with models wearing shorter-than-short dresses and dancing provocatively.

This is an eye-gate which needs to be closed.

Storing Information

Memory plays a huge role in our intellectual and physical activity. In humans—far more than other species—the processing of information goes beyond receiving and coding input.

Data is processed by the mind in stages. For example,

NEW MIND! MEMORY VERSE #43

My soul, wait thou only upon God; for my expectation is from him.

– PSALM 62:5

when you hear music, the information is saved like a tape recorder stores sound. Although your ears hear the tones, it sends the waves to our brain to be processed and stockpiled.

Based on how important it is to you, or how many times you hear it, the sounds are stored in either short term or long term memory.

We've all heard songs we didn't particularly care for at first. However, the more we listen, the harder it is to get the tune out of our mind. We are hooked! Before we know it, we find ourselves actually falling in love with some crazy song!

WHAT WE SPEND OUR TIME DWELLING ON IS THE VERY THING WE EVENTUALLY ACT OUT.

"I'm Losing My Mind!"

What we spend our time dwelling on is the very thing we eventually act out. As King Solomon wrote, *"For as he thinketh in his heart, so is he"* (Proverbs 23:7).

The person who constantly *imagines* he is sick will not only begin to feel ill, he can actually *become* sick.

Just as we take our car in for a tuneup, our mind also

119

NEW MIND! MEMORY VERSE #44

Give, and it will be given to you. A good measure, pressed down, shaken together and running over, will be poured into your lap. For with the measure you use, it will be measured to you.

– Luke 6:38 NIV

NEW MIND! NEW YOU!

needs renewing. We need to flush out the impurities and fill it with what is new and fresh—the incomparable Word of God.

Some people, overcome with the pressures of life, in desperation exclaim, "I'm losing my mind!" The apostle Paul tells us how to protect our thinking. He writes, *"Be careful for nothing; but in every thing by prayer and supplication with thanksgiving let your requests be made known unto God. And the peace of God, which passeth all understanding, shall keep your hearts and minds through Christ Jesus"* (Philippians 4:6-7).

Next, we are given a valuable list with which we should fill our mind. *"Finally, brethren, whatsoever things are true, whatsoever things are honest, whatsoever things are pure, whatsoever things are lovely, whatsoever things are of good report; if there be any virtue, and if there be any praise, think on these things"* (Philippians 4:6-8).

A Conscious Effort

Focusing on things of "good report" involves a deliberate act of your will—a conscious effort. This also includes giving God praise for the positive things which occur in your life.

NEW MIND! MEMORY VERSE #45

For ye are bought with a price: therefore glorify God in your body, and in your spirit, which are God's.

– 1 CORINTHIANS 6:20

When this happens, you can say with Paul, *"I know both how to be abased, and know how to abound: every where and in all things I am instructed both to be full and to be hungry, both to abound and to suffer need. I can do all things through Christ which strengthens me"* (Philippians 4:12-13).

Sure, we all have good days and bad, yet with the renewing of our mind we no longer center our thoughts on the negative. God has so much more in store.

The Key to Deliverance

Until our minds are renewed, we can be free, yet not delivered. The children of Israel are a good example.

Although God had freed them out of the bondage of Egypt, they wandered in the wilderness for 40 years—and only a handful made it to the Promised Land. Again and

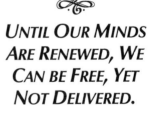

UNTIL OUR MINDS ARE RENEWED, WE CAN BE FREE, YET NOT DELIVERED.

again, they grumbled about their condition and told Moses, *"Would God that we had died in the land of Egypt!... And wherefore hath the Lord brought us unto this land, to fall by the sword, that our wives and our*

New Mind! Memory Verse #46

Without faith it is impossible to please him: for he that cometh to God must believe that he is, and that he is a rewarder of them that diligently seek him.

– HEBREWS 11:6

children should be a prey? were it not better for us to return into Egypt?"(Numbers 14:3,4).

By looking at only the present, they totally blocked the miracles of the exodus from their memory:

- They were led with a pillar of cloud by day and fire by night (Exodus 13:21-22).
- God parted the seas and they crossed on dry ground (Exodus 14:21-22).
- They were fed with manna from heaven (Exodus 16:13-36).
- They drank from water which sprang out of a rock (Exodus 17:5-6).

Yes, they were in the wilderness, but thank God they weren't in Egypt!

You're a Victor!

Satan will deliberately cause you to waste so much time on your problems you can't see how far you have actually come. If you haven't arrived in your land of promise, praise God anyhow!

It is time to discard a victim mentality. You're not a victim; you are a *victor!* Jesus declares, *"Behold, I give unto you power to tread on serpents and scorpions, and over all the power of the enemy: and nothing shall by any means hurt you"* (Luke 10:19 KJV).

Who is such power for? *You!*

You have authority over the enemy: *"And they overcame him by the blood of the lamb, and by the word of their testimony"* (Revelation 12:11).

Is your testimony one of a powerful child of God, or are you still feeling sorry for yourself, moaning, "Poor old me!"?

"Needles and Pins"

I grew up watching Jackie Gleason on *The Honeymooners.* In one episode in his role as Ralph Kramden, he went to the doctor because of his stress, The physician told Ralph, "The next time something gets you upset, begin to say, "Pins and needles, needles and pins, a happy man is a man that grins!"

If that sounds childish, try this: "He has made me glad. He has made me glad. I will rejoice for He has made me glad!"

These simple words can turn your day from pressure to His perfect peace.

No More Excuses

Stop seeing yourself as defeated and weak. Instead, stand on this divine promise: *"...they that wait upon the Lord shall renew their strength: they shall mount up with wings as eagles; they shall run, and not be weary; and they shall walk, and not faint"* (Isaiah 40:31).

Bury your excuses and ask the Lord to be permanently *"renewed in the spirit of your mind"* (Ephesians 4:23).

If not today, when? If not you, then who?

CHAPTER 8

IT'S ALREADY DONE!

The idea of having a new mind is not a far-fetched concept based on supposition. It is reality, based on the authority of scripture.

The moment you ask God's Son to forgive you of your sin, you become a totally new person: *"Therefore if any man be in Christ, he is a new creature: old things are passed away; behold, all things are become new"* (2 Corinthians 5:17).

The born again experience is not the result of anything we have done, rather it is because of what the Lord has already accomplished. He not only exchanges our old heart, but also our mind. As a believer, *"we have*

NEW MIND! MEMORY VERSE #47

*But the Comforter, which
is the Holy Ghost, whom the
Father will send in my name,
he shall teach you all things,
and bring all things to your
remembrance, whatsoever
I have said unto you.*

– JOHN 14:26

the mind of Christ" (1 Corinthians 2:16).

It's Accomplished

What the Lord promises is not only designated for the future, it is for the present! He doesn't tell us we *will* have these things—we *have* them now. As Paul writes, *"Therefore being justified by faith, we have peace with God through our Lord Jesus Christ"* (Romans 5:1).

The change in our circumstances through the renewing of our mind has already taken place!

I pray the Lord will open our eyes to this understanding and give us a revelation of this divine truth. To some it may seem impossible, *"But God hath chosen the foolish things of the world to confound the wise; and God hath chosen the weak things of the world to confound the things which are mighty"*(1 Corinthians1:27).

When I first came to the Lord, one of the greatest barriers to my faith was realizing what I was praying for had already been completed at the cross.

He Doesn't Sleep

In the creation story, we read on the seventh day God rested, yet this doesn't mean He is still up in the heavens

NEW MIND! MEMORY VERSE #48

And he said to them all, If any man will come after me, let him deny himself, and take up his cross daily, and follow me.

– LUKE 9:23

sleeping! No. The Bible tells us, *"he that keepeth Israel shall neither slumber nor sleep"* (Psalm 121:4).

Our Heavenly Father is constantly watching over His children.

You are Pre-Approved

Let me give you this illustration. A friend may call you at work and say, "I made you an apple pie. Why don't you pick it up on the way home?"

If you were delayed leaving your job, or had a bad day at the office and decided to head straight home, guess what: the pie is still waiting for you!

Even after you took a shower and went to bed—the pie is still there. It has been baked, and it's yours.

HE THOUGHT OF YOUR DESIRES LONG BEFORE YOU WERE EVER BORN.

God's gift has also been prepared. He thought of your desires long before you were ever born: *"For whom he did foreknow, he also did predestinate to be conformed to the image of his Son"* (Romans 8:29).

He pre-approved of your needs—your job, your house, your healing. It is already done!

NEW MIND! MEMORY VERSE #49

*In my Father's house
are many mansions: if
it were not so, I would
have told you. I go to
prepare a place for you.
And if I go and prepare a
place for you, I will come
again, and receive you unto
myself; that where I am,
there ye may be also.*

– JOHN 14:2-3

Receive It!

Christ took our sins to the cross and *"by whose stripes ye were healed"* (1 Peter 2:24). That is past tense—your miracle has happened! All you have to do is reach out and accept it!

Even more, we can be *"confident of this very thing, that he which hath begun a good work in you will perform it until the day of Jesus Christ"* (Philippians 1:6).

Because you *were* changed, you will *stay* changed!

Greater Works!

When you know you have already won the battle, it makes no sense to consider defeat. While others are discussing the loss of their jobs, you are talking about a raise! When the world speaks of doom and destruction, you are claiming triumph.

Remember the words of Jesus: *"Verily, verily, I say unto you, He that believeth on me, the works that I do shall he do also; and greater works than these shall he do; because I go unto my father"* (John 14:12).

You have the confidence that *"greater is he that is in you, than he that is in the world"* (1 John 4:4).

NEW MIND! MEMORY VERSE #50

They that wait upon the Lord shall renew their strength; they shall mount up with wings as eagles; they shall run, and not be weary; and they shall walk, and not faint.

– ISAIAH 40:31

Above, Not Beneath!

Whatever your dreams and goals, be determined that with God's help you will live in excellence. Rest in this assurance, *"And the Lord shall make thee plenteous in goods, in the fruit of thy body, and in the fruit of thy cattle, and in the fruit of thy ground, in the land which the Lord sware unto thy fathers to give thee"* (Deuteronomy 28:11).

There is even more! *"The Lord shall open unto thee his good treasure, the heaven to give the rain unto thy land in his season, and to bless all the work of thine hand: and thou shalt lend unto many nations, and thou shalt not borrow. And the Lord shall make thee the head, and not the tail; and thou shalt be above only, and thou shalt not be beneath; if that thou hearken unto the commandments of the Lord thy God, which I command thee this day, to observe and to do them"* (vv.12-13).

What a covenant He has made with you!

Simply Answer

Praise God, we are standing on the promises the Father has already spoken into our lives. When we have the mind of Christ, it's not our efforts, but *His* grace which allows us to walk in His blessings and favor.

NEW MIND! MEMORY VERSE #51

*Delight thyself also
in the Lord; and he shall
give thee the desires
of thine heart.*

– PSALM 37:4

NEW MIND! NEW YOU!

All you are required to do is answer the call of God on your life: *"Ask, and it shall be given you; seek, and ye shall find; knock, and it shall be opened unto you: For every one that asketh receiveth; and he that seeketh findeth, and to him that knocketh it shall be opened"* (Matthew 7:7-8).

Even before you receive the answer, believe it is yours. *"Through faith we understand that the worlds were framed by the word of God, so that things which are seen were not made of things which do appear"* (Hebrews 11:3).

> **EVEN BEFORE YOU RECEIVE THE ANSWER, BELIEVE IT IS YOURS.**

His miracle-working power is at work!

God's Directive

It is my earnest prayer this book will be a life-changing experience. This will happen when you make a total commitment to memorize the 52 scriptures on these pages.

Please don't take this lightly. It is God's divine directive. He says, *"These commandments that I give you today are to be upon your hearts. Impress them on your children. Talk about them when you sit at home and*

NEW MIND! MEMORY VERSE #52

Rejoice in the Lord always. I will say it again: Rejoice!

– PHILIPPIANS 4:4 NIV

when you walk along the road, when you lie down and when you get up" (Deuteronomy 6:6-7 NIV).

Start today to meditate on the Word. Repeat the passages out loud, pray them silently and allow the Holy Spirit to make them come alive.

Oh, what a difference it makes when you are saturated with scripture. Your thoughts, words and actions will not only be transformed, they will fulfill the Father's purpose for your future.

You will have a new heart, soul and mind—resulting in a brand new you!

FOR A COMPLETE LIST OF RESOURCES
BY THE AUTHOR OR TO SCHEDULE SPEAKING
ENGAGEMENTS, CONTACT:

BISHOP WAYLYN HOBBS, JR.
CONEY ISLAND CATHEDRAL OF DELIVERANCE
2816 MERMAID AVENUE
BROOKLYN, NY 11224

PHONE: 718-946-5913
INTERNET:
www.waylynhobbsjrministries.com